A Watchful Astronomy

for my mother

A Watchful Astronomy
Paul Deaton

Seren is the book imprint of
Poetry Wales Press Ltd.
57 Nolton Street, Bridgend, Wales, CF31 3AE
www.serenbooks.com
facebook.com/SerenBooks
twitter@SerenBooks

The right of Paul Deaton to be identified as
the author of this work has been asserted in accordance
with the Copyright, Designs and Patents Act, 1988.

ISBN: 978-1-78172-407-1
ebook: 978-1-78172-402-6
Kindle: 978-1-78172-403-3

A CIP record for this title is available from the British Library.

The publisher acknowledges the financial assistance of the Welsh Books Council.

Cover Photograph: Earthrise – Apollo 8 © NASA

Printed by Airdrie Print Services Ltd.

Contents

II

A Watchful Astronomy

Quarter cupped in the black velvet, a moon.
December days sweep through,
morning fogs chloroform the speechless spectral trees,
they come to slowly out of wind-threshed dreams
black and dark. You work. Do what you need to do
but always with one eye on the lean-to sky.

Walking home, over Gaol Ferry Bridge,
after some party drinks, Orion splayed
above St Paul's Church like a fat limbed gingerbread man,
and that star, cold as quartz, your watchful astronomy
tells you isn't a star but giant Jupiter, up there,
the same size as the stone in your shoe.

In Front of the Rock Garden

– self-portrait aged 2½ –

Everything about me is perfect pose,
for my mother, my mother's gaze.
I'm looking straight at camera
but in an ambivalent, must-I, way;

not sure of the setting, nor my part.
There's something strange, something large
left unexplained I'm trying to frame;
wary tilt of my sun-soaked quizzical head.

An ageless question?
Who is me and who the not me?
Already I hold tight my right to silence. To abstain.
Already I forbear. This life struggle will never be easy.

Behind my back my hands
twisting each wrist in Chinese burns.

Lear Father

He weighs your disloyalty on you like Lear.
It's not him: heavy, hard and incorrigible,
but you in all you do. You are the breaker
of rites, of bond. But let's set this true;
to be yourself is *de facto*, to let him down.
Inverted. It's the wrong way round.
Oh, God, how many years has it taken to see
the devices, the instruments of what this man
would not do; captive by non-loving,
your youth, your life, held within his frown;
this man, your father, the acts of a nowhere clown.
And the truth you didn't see. He had no truck
with you. It's not you he sees. He takes you,
takes everything to the source from which he bleeds.

Sea Bream Dinner

And sometimes it is enough to only
think about what to have for dinner,
and to go out to the shops in advance
through the square beneath the lurching
horse chestnuts, and over the long broken
path slabs at midday, to buy fish, fresh
from the fishmonger's magician
hands and to get home in the evening,
to cook with stained spoon and heavy pan
what has been found first by a Cornish fisherman.

And not to be in a devil's rush, not to high
hurdle against the odds a sprinter's dinner,
but to gas light the stove, to put
the whole sea bream in the clay tagine
carefully, as if it were your own parents
you were laying to rest, with sprig
of bay, splash of wine, slide this day's death
into the oven with a softly worded message,
be wholesome, silver sea thing,
treasured, let the white meat do its best.

Polish

My mother always tip-top shiny
like the silverware, the copper
pans, the brass wall plates
she'd polish and polish again,
best side out, always gleaming
like a glowing hub-cap moon.

My mother always bright-eyed
quickly on the side of life,
that it's ok, who she is, appears.
The luminous life she loves.
Her unspoken line;
life is light and only then it's right.

Though I know well and it's possible to tell
from her stripped cuticles,
her nervous not-sitting-still,
that there's some fretful paddling,
panicked flapping beneath her glide,
that polished outer shiny side.

Home

Walk the bike up Church Lane and leave the pub
to shrink into the grubby dark. Hit that length of unlit
street where the houses still swim in a wartime blackout
and feel yourself at once alone, that stranger
in the self the darkness brings you back to:
not your day now, but this sixth sense to follow home.
Climb three score steps to the summit of the hill,
at the top turn left past the gothic mansion pile,
tender touch the jasmine's lace-white stars crocheting the wall.
At the single streetlight spotting the pavement
like it's an empty stage, pass up the offer
of a monologue, with 'no comment'. Nearly home.
Trundle the bike between two rows of tucked-tight sleeping cars.
Are you glad of your life? Tonight you are.

Llanddeusant

The chapel crouches slack,
broken backed on the verge wall.
Too many years of sky sinking
stone. Cloud weight.

Behind, Carmarthen Fan climbs
with low, swollen mounds
before a shear crag wall
of tooth toppled sandstone.

Mid Wales recumbent.
A lane winds in past the last lonely farm,
bounding over the parish like the band
around a tennis ball.

The whole world is backed away
to those who shut doors
on everything but the land, seeing
more clearly than anyone that here lies their raft.

Night. And the stone sputtered valley,
rent by the filter brook.
Here, a private audience,
this speechless stand of stars.

Morning. The clouds are tower
stacked, ashen demolitions rising
from the south as though the colliers'
cottage fires, valley hidden, still burned.

Starlings

in the lone evening: flooding, falling, flocking,
with locked-out wings, flasher's black macs,
stretched to the tip. Taut batman capes.
They glide and weave, cutting chutes,

curves, into cloudy city skies. One favourite tree
across the street; there they roost seasonally.
My trilling friends. My loyal morning roof callers.
Pulled me through winter to spring.

My early evening railing spirits. My tall
tree trumpeters. My end-of-work signallers.
Boy, they know how to sing. The why of starling?
Continually in receipt of life's good news.

What is it they say? Absolutely it's no secret.
Each day is match day.

The Spin

I remember going to the park with my father,
at the bottom of Harnham Hill –
not something we often did, ever did;
we trailed down the chalky banks, cloistered
with beech and hallways of maroon earth,
near the steep flexed road, where once, on black ice,
on the way to school, the Cortina
spun a complete three sixty; for me,
my sister, our necks swivelled, pin eyes
growing to the size of barn owls', heads out
on bent stems leaning forward from the car.
It was the highlight of the year, of any year,
I, six, stomach senses keen but not yet knowing,
she, eight, red hair, frizzy, showering like a meteor.

Books

You never said much; never expanded
into a raft of words, even though you'd read,
you bragged, every novel in our local library.
Saturday mornings as you flipped each page
I'd muster six lines to your one.
Dad, I couldn't even get you to say
if they were any good.
Nothing got higher marks
than a bother-me-not-shrug. Bad looks.
'It was alright,' you'd wearingly say.
Books. I failed to fathom why you read them.
Living with you wasn't happy. It was hard.
And it seems this was the world you wanted;
a cottage, a hovel, a room in the dark.

He's

old before his time stuck in his chair.
Thunder like thunder. Will it won't it arrive?
Bitter as burnt bacon rind.
Crooked as the cat and impossible to read.
Always descending, cyclonic, coming
on strong, a low Atlantic front. Polar.
Heavy on the air. No safety catch,
an old gun with one last shot.
Impenetrable as a forest and as silent.

Quick to bring to the boil.
Quick to scold. Hot yet always cold.
Bursts like lava to instantly harden.
Frozen as the furthest star, light-years away.
A woodsman; sawing and chopping,
splitting the grain, the family strain.
Gated, medieval, with few ways in.
Short on views.
A land where it's always raining.

Stalker

The moon comes knocking on our door;
a slavish stalker who hangs around all night.
The slowest and subtlest of walkers, he matched
at an equal distance each of our homeward steps.

We close our door on him, push him out
only to find he's already skirted the house,
taken the side alley, slipped the padlocked gate,
jumped the flowerpots and several four-foot pine
and is staring fixedly through our unlit bedroom windows.

He'll watch all night, like this, through
his scarf of cloud, the broken drape;
while we count faceless sheep he waits.
He holds the hours we conflate.

The night marked down to his pinpoint satisfaction
he lets us go though we'll never know
at what thin hour he left.
It's been this way all month.

Inselberg Father

His shape abutted like the looming Inselbergs:
grey, dark and unyielding.
On good days a rose light sparked over him,
set him off in the setting sun, ignited his upper flanks,
softened the cliffs, enlarged his own magnificence.

He carried my life before him like an erratic boulder.
This man I couldn't fathom. He said he was
needless of love, but this did not set me free.
There is a scored grain in the terraced Torridonian rocks,
eight hundred million years old, chiselled and filed by ice.

His shape was large, brooding, like Suilven,
Cul Mor, Stac Pollaidh: held its form
even in the dark of night, loomed larger,
reared over the coastal crofts
and repulsed the low Lewisian land to the lip of the sea.

That Bang

I curl in bed like an ammonite,
thinking what valleys my ribs will leave
in the mattress soft sediment.

The exposed contours of bones
linked like the constellations of stars.
Here lies my foot,

the half-moon bay of my hunter's heel.
My skull a deflated football,
thin as bird-broken eggshell.

I wish to descend,
see life in the era of ferns,
pre-school, pre-man.

Yet time is travelling the wrong way.
Some say it is speeding up.
Those from Cambridge;

physics and the universe's tidal outwash flow.
That Big Bang.
Louder than an Alpine thunderclap.

I hold the space between stars.
The hour's no-hour.
And, as in alleyways, I hold too, the concentrated blackness.

Victoria Park

The trees transfixed. The whole long line of limes
parade through the park. Here they dug down,
grew strong. Here and only here they homed in.

Lost or stuck to a last move. A black square,
this bald-board, this open ground,
this park on a city's hill.

The game doesn't complete.
It will always be your turn in your world.
Always tea-break. Always unfinished.

Life is paradox. The towering trees, the plum-pinned night,
this slope of static kings,
this world you walk through never to be solved.

School Days

All through secondary school
Dad came home from work starkly depressed.
How easily life is defined by someone else's stress.
Eight sugared coffees weren't enough to lift him.

He'd stare into his mug of Nescafé
the way some people draw down the moon.
Me and my sister, we knew what to do.
We walked a wide berth around him.

Not much a father more a wounded bear:
shackled to work, the mortgage, a nudging wife, suburban rooms.
He mauled us with his gloom
and we never did learn what had truly stung him.

Shoemaker Father

You were an electrical engineer: fixing, finding,
fudging, taking things apart, making things do;
washing machines, toasters, car radiators.
With you, mechanical objects had more than nine lives,
weren't left to die, you stretched out time, the failings
of hard used, beaten, chore-full lives.
Always found a way. The bits and bobs:
screws, wires, clips, frames, cluttering the kitchen table.
Perhaps it was the only time you were happy?
But in the tradition of Grimm, of fairy tale, I'd say
you were a shoemaker. You had needles
not for sewing, but stitching; hooked and large.
How could you mend so many things: shoes, carpets,
leather belts, bags, wallets, while the family fell apart.

Playing Dead

There were two of them, of course,
always pulling two opposite ways;
never together, never in harmony.
Mum heaving her half, collapsing us,
dad declaiming what she'd do undone.
My sister got out. Left home at sixteen.
Sped away defiantly with a black-bearded
man astride the back of his red Honda 500cc.
Me? My life went weightless, a slow spiral
to the outer galaxy; all communications cut;
spinning some solipsistic silent scream,
not fight or flight; adrift and zombie.
Playing dead was no way to split the scene.

Walls

It's been a year for walls, their slow creeping
and bowing; a feather crack peels apart
like a broken zip; as if these bricks and stones
have heard a rumour, learnt of their imprisonment,
refuse the collective, the hard line,
the spirit-levelled edge, the soil-starved
passivity of wall.

The butcher's one at the back of my flat,
the bricks rippled like a jolting current
has flailed through, or it's had one too many,
keels like the boys that blindly waver home.
The full taproot crack, as if someone had hit
it squarely with an axe, its split spine parting,
won't ever join back.

Then there's the high wall to the parkland court,
a huddle of caveman-coarse stones
near the top seized their chance, jumped,
no matter how high the drop, 'sod it' they cried
late one January night, 'jump now or we die';
no longer able to defend the long, ludicrous
premise of wall.

And this one last, inside, is ours to shift;
we slip from pasts slowly, what
was rigged, the walls our parents built us;
our schools, then jobs, unknowingly fixed,
no matter how firmly and securely;
searching after all these years
for our own rough ground.

Star Bound

The day hangs in the balance.
Autumn's untethered world is suspended;
neither sunshine nor the turmoil
of sweeping, scavenging winds.
The sky is faultless. Pig-rind clean.

On a day like today it is possible to surmise
the earth tilts forward on its axis, lopsided
by 23 degrees, like the simple down and up
of my Turkish, handheld cast iron scales,
cantilevered by a bar no longer
than a pencil, and we are
making for shadows and the winter's
long night outer galaxy traverse.

I stop short. If you were here
I would admit I cannot stand straight. I bend.
I am tilting like the earth
through autumn's inclined day glow,
here too to make a life's traverse
through the quiet, icy terraces of night.

Streets

Each morning momentarily as I rode to school
I searched a corner house's blinds
to spy, in the sunken gloom, one long settee,
a listing dresser, painted crockery,
sometimes the flicker of a mute TV
before the road ducked left as if permanently redirected.

Where we lived there was no great escape;
our lives were sealed by planner's tarmac,
cracked, pitched pavements, grey-end walls
lacking windows, dark Welsh slate.
In the terraced suburbs we were met with unplaceable sunsets.
We forgot the earth is round.

Slad House

We viewed an old stone house in Slad
in the basin of a steep-sided valley.
The garden a ruin, and damp, an always-damp,
from the shade of the tall trees,
the shadow of the hill. A lawn of liverworts,
the green algae path ice-rink skiddy. The estate agent,
old blethering bloke that he was, wouldn't shut up,
warbled like some record-stuck bird.

Worn, heavy front step, a pantry,
a wash house, crooked stairs
to a buckled landing,
panes of glass where spiders slept.

We could have gone to ground,
let the moss grow over us, our final blanket:
buy it, a simple choice, and no one would have
heard from us again; decades, quarter centuries,
the deaths of widows, men home from war,
are as nothing to gone-to-earth houses, the hard-paced
twenty-first century, no more than a memory,
our time marked by the growing stains of lichen on a wall.

Owl

I shuffle between rooms because I can't sleep
and I think of the owl I listened to on Dartmoor
flitting between branches, climbing the clumpy valley,
invisible in darkness, announcing each move
with a sharp ker-wick that grew louder,
traversing the row of river-tied trees and me,
in the field's edge, risen to night and sharp-eared,
listening until it landed on the lame, lopped holly,
now near and present as though
it had landed on my own right shoulder.

And, as I stoop in darkness between doorways,
wishing I was asleep, mind-mysterious,
head pitching like a hand-held lamp;
I wonder: what tree or branch was I vainly looking for?
The owl flew on with a silk-slow hush;
a cape sweep of unclasped wings.
And I knew I had been left by a creature
who knows the nights' hollows better than me:
can let go into the dimness, unperturbed,
can find in the black blindness what it needs to find.

Call

Dad phones – it's unexpected – he never phones.
'How are you?' I say.
A stilted exchange, my reserve grown thick,
diffident, between us an unbridgeable
gorge gap. What is it we lack?
Two people who long ago lost the ends
of the father–son thread, the power to connect.
'The operation's Friday the twelfth.
Back for Xmas (*hollow pause*) maybe.'
'Are you nervous?' 'No,' he blanks. He's 'ok'.
'Look after mum,' he intones, dry as a bone.
That's it, more or less, no other words.
I'm on the phone but I look away.
He never did make Christmas day.

December

dawn rakes
the land's ashen carpets
and the sun's cranberry coal
glisters low in the grate.

The tree in the backyard
is black capillaried,
the upmost branches
a thicket of primed spears.

The laden sky trundles
labouringly as a coal lorry,
with brimful clouds,
black and bagged.

For a while the morning hesitates,
anciently, then demists.
The lanes into the country
are thick and dark.

The Coffin Hut

The house is watched by the moon.
Here above the Summer Isles,
stretched like dormant black cats,
it has found an honest face to steer by.

We have slept a night
and the whole sky has cartwheeled over us.
The stars, like workmen leaving a shift,
broke the gates and just plain wandered off.

The sniper sun crests the snowy hill,
threads the dawn and, like an opened
oven door, warms the waking moor.
Six tall pines tingle and purl,

and the pine needles chilblain.
They've grown protective
of the house and no longer
yearn for the forest.

Confirmed in clear ground,
here they will end their days.
The back of the snubbed barn,
shouldered another cold night.

Even if the house cannot love the barn,
it being the crofters' coffin hut,
the sun at least
gives the iced stones a warmed arm.

Year's End

The year's fire is spent.
Over the Usk crowding clouds,
a whole flotilla, race at pace.
Walking off Tor y Foel the light loiters
breaks on hunched horizons.
We halt, angled against wind,
the day's change and the lessening luminosity.
The year backs into darkness.
The hills hold a vow of silence.
Stood above the Tinkertoy farms
has it always been like this?
Time living but immutably fixed.
Earth tan and dun-coloured.
There is now no sap. No blood.
Long tailed tits flitter away.
The winds whip up autumn's ashes;
smear them rudely into dark-cheeked clouds.
We wander the late year's stony chill
and fear we'll never be warm again.
The sun's fire flickering out:
the months, the seasons, time itself,
burnt down to blackout.

Estuary Winds

The earth and sky suggest
everything has gone into
winter's blue whale dive.

The land a cold neighbour
holding breath
for one palpable deep duration.

Rogue winds take advantage of un-summered space:
skirl like broiling birds and force fingers
into the hollow of a gatepost

playing an eerie flute
to the thin line of beech trees
at the high point of the field's curtain.

They then assault a clump
of stencilled trees sticking up,
centre field, like headdress plumes

from a more stately time,
or maybe the trees, holding firm,
have trapped the winds like fish

in one final struggle,
the last moment of their migratory lives,
netted and outwitted in skeletal branches.

On the Severn's mist glassed horizon those still free
are etching with rain,
cutting a winter's lithograph in hair-breadth scars.

Christmas

You bought the presents your tight budget allowed,
had a third and fourth date with the RAF girl from match.com
spent several hours on Somerset's M5,
watched the weather pendulum from bright blue
to a filthy hue; climbed the chill hills
of Cribyn, Pen y Fan, Corn Du,
to better know you were alive;
sighted Saturn several pre-dawn mornings,
when the world was black and still.
Ran a race New Year's day – the hangover 10k –
and did better than ok. Gone in a flash, crushed
Christmas's silver-starred wrapping paper
into the bleak black bins outside;
settled back for work and another year's streaming tide.

New Year's Walk

Quell the day's work with a stiff, swift drink.
Lift the limp leather jacket, hung
from the hook in the hall and quick saunter
one late last lap around the block;
climb the brow of Mendip Road,
and wade into a flooded field of stars.
Hear for the day's first time
the audible beating of your heart.
Wander down to the uncurtained house
showing all, view the globe paper shade
bright and bold as last month's moon,
drop past the poorly peopled pub.
At the Shang-Hai takeaway turn sharp left;
stroll back along the terraced rows of dim-lit homes.
Near your own back gate, outstare the frozen
caught-in-the-act black cat.
Now at your door, slip back the lock
and climb the wooden stair,
walk gently into the first few steps of another year.

DIY

In the weeks before Dad died
time suddenly seemed to speed up,
the counting clock came at him in a rush.
We watched him scurry about. Stood aside.
Down at 3 a.m. to finish painting mum's utility room,
then straight on, before dawn, to the closet loo.
DIY the goodbye tasks he had to do.
I knew what was coming and somehow he did too.
Round at my sister's with tools in hand,
to fit an alarm – they clashed – his trademark bitter reprimand.
He turned up at my house too, when I hadn't asked;
and I wasn't sure what he needed to do;
bent double, unplugging the dodgy sink.
It was all black and final as the registry ink.

High in Hanham

My mate Dave in front.
I purr-past Dave going up the wooded hill.
Those bloody concrete giant's steps.
The guy in front is, well, in front.
I peg it alongside the Avon slick as Swarfega.
Dave tracks me.
The tall poplars, shimmering quill feathers.
The yellow brick towpath winds away.
Back in the woods climbing the hill Dave whips past.
For a moment I reckon we can both catch the 2nd place guy
but that is hubris, a fading false hope.
Dave stretches his gain, flickering away like a fish.
We hit the rope tied to the bank
like a crocodile slipway and haul up.
That's me all in. Buried and gone.
Dave's off across the footie field killing it,
wild helicopter arms. There's no stopping him.
The sun's a citrine blaze beyond the trees.
Casts a winter wax on everything.
I lap the field nonchalantly. Haloed.
Time to cruise to the finish like I wasn't even trying!
That sun. That lemon glaze.
In the rec's bar afterwards it's on everything:
carrot cake, circle of friends, crap carpet.

Worlebury Woods, January

It is the dirty time of year.
Winter's aftermath hangs a soot print
on the landscape. The roads crushed
to peppercorn dust by three weeks' ice.
Grit grindings are flecked in fences,
grass verges and into the bleached fields.
January. And there is nothing that the earth will not stick to,
thrown across damp swathes of Somerset sedge.
A near dark born from the perpetually wet,
the reduction of matter, of last year's life
channelled and re-channelled
into the rivers, the drains and the rhynes.

Up on the hill, Worlebury Woods stand silent,
the trees like cattle taking the mizzle wet.
Cobwebs canopy the branches
as though it were a tropic rainforest
and the ancient snake Severn retracts,
rather than visit the harbour
the left-for-dead hotels,
so far out it may be gone for days
and the muddy pavement that it leaves
no one knows what to do with,
though the wading birds wide stride and lance it.

The day fails to reach any surface,
smothered in its white plastic bag and the sun
is a distant neoprene glow from another world.
Car careering home, out of the levels,
overladen clouds slug out the lost byways.
Back in the forest, the trunks are darkened,
long thin necks run cold and stained with rain.

Fallen Night

All night the winds strike the sides
of the come-on-then-I-can-take-it house.
The sash windows struggle and strive
like live bait, wanting to break free from their frames.
But the winds surge again and again;
unleash their hurly hysteria hour on hour.
This February fallen night, without borders
or boundaries. I think of street chaos:
Cairo, Croydon or Rome, looters,
bloodletters, a world misinterpreted;
the winds a siege to our duck-downed heads.

The early morning radio details the aftermath:
gales scoured the north and lowlands of Scotland,
road closures, slates down, pines uprooted
and what will be, for sleepy ears: a man's
anonymous death; a car tree-struck, and a life taken.
And I think, soberly, in the safety of our home,
these pistons of earth are real then,
shuddering the stone, this is the dark chance of life;
the brief intersecting moment, the way fate finds us,
with love or with ill. The future flung
though air; an ash or an oak,
uprooted in gales, with our name on it.

Not Winter

The sky muddies to a river's silt wash
and the sodden earth lies smudged
in the dawn dampness of late February;
and all we have to show for the struggle
of neutered, suspenseful weeks
are a few thrust daffodil spears,
a few small blown bulbs of snowdrops,
porcelain-pure, crouched huddled
and shivering at the lane side,
while above their midst
a stoned-rubbed blur of Mendip Hills.

This hugging winter greatcoat continues,
clads us for days, with a vanquished still air,
and we could believe we are at sea,
with no wind on the sail, can go nowhere;
stuck in self-same weeks that flow out
through the dark curve of sun-shy space.
This Atlantic drift that tows us through the mute
months, though, is not now winter, is not the river's
entombed death bed, stacked with bronze-black leaves,
but is, in fact, (can we bear it)
from the shaded silent pools, the start of life.

Black Knight

A few forgotten objects Dad passed on:
copperplate pens with long nail nibs,
still stained black, one coal-fire red,
laid to rest
for twenty years in the shed's office chest;

a Monopoly set
yanked by a seaman uncle from his sinking merchant ship
U-boat torpedoed
at the beginning of the Second World War,
but minus the board;

the pine-green balsa houses, the pink, prim hotels
strewn on the field of our living-room floor,
much else that was yours:
the board, this uncle and your gambling father,
we never saw.

And the chess pieces we played and played;
of our two wooden box sets, the best
hand carved, you varnished and weighted with lead.
The black knight like you
could lose its head.

II

Raskolnikov

Each day you accumulate small steals from hard efforts
and the spirit's degradation stretches out its black wing.

The heart sours as it grows, sickens like forgotten fruit
when it fails to bring forth. Nobody knows you.

How heavy time is. You think that's axiomatic.
Death struggle in the mind's vortex. You wait to be found out.

Can the stem hold the weight of the head –
the promissory seeds show a leaning but no ground?

You winter in self-mutterings, climb the fateful stair,
then money, like life, a caterwaul reflex, empties all away.

You raise the axe a hundred thousand times;
hear the whistle of air, expect everything to burn and smoke,

show its disease, the earth go down in an iron flame,
but not this, this slow summer smoulder,

not the equitable light, not the re-dawning day after
day over the Neva, the Voznesensky bridge,

not the suffering streets, the people like lice zigzagging,
not down every Prospekt this inscrutable vice holding the same.

What you carry came before your birth.
You disappoint yourself. All else is a fever of the sun.

Spring Tide

Slow revolutions and slow orbits.
Venus in view
bullet-bright
bores the black horizon.

These are the stellar cycles.
The day's deep turning.
The planets pull past.
Jupiter. Venus. Then Mars

conjunct with Uranus.
The parting faces of the moon.
An eclipse. Shadow on the sun.
The tide thick and slow.

Life learns its quiet phases.
We draw close and then, it seems,
with no power of our own
pull apart. Find new orbits.

Patterns of sameness
yet nothing stays the same.
Days decay. There is no way
of taking the distance out of the distance.

Such a small back door to shut out
the crowding stadium of stars.
The venetian blinds stay up.
Outside the silence doesn't sleep.

Spring

The sparrows banter in the bushes
that crowd the walls
of the World's End alleyway
as I walk to the library.

There is, it seems, much to catch up on.
Winter was bitter cold;
five months that had us by the throat,
five months in our house that were bone lonely.

April. And earth is touched
by the hand of a new sun.
A sun, from its stoked store,
that wants to warm us,

pulls at zips, unbuttons a thick-coated
Saxon taciturn resistance.
The releasing rays bring back lost leisure:
walking back home, in the dry dust

of my road, a black and white tabby
reclines, eyes me disdainfully
with the look of a Cleopatra
on an invisible chaise longue.

Words

Late afternoon I speak to Mum on the phone;
she's sorting through her past,
four hundred or so odd-sized photographs.
'Well, you won't want to do it,'
she says, 'when I'm gone,
I won't leave you that task.'
We switch tack, not from fear,
from silent truth, what can't come back.
We talk of mulish rough weather,
April squalls, the wind's choking embrace
of a newly dressed willow, bringing it down,
its road wreckage near her place.
Dad's death was like that tree.
She talks in tangents. Is this what she means?

Cake

Because Mum didn't let us when we were young
– it was her special thing to bake a cake –
I went once when she was seventy-two.
'Get the bowls out,' I said, 'the sugar,
the eggs, the flour, those unused
treacle-stained spoons;
let's bake a cake,
today together,
share and show just once
the truth of what you do.'
It's not enough and was never enough back then,
I realised, three decades late,
thumbing my book on classic cakes,
to only lick the spoon.

This Easter

The tall trunked beeches stagger up the hill.
They've been doing it for years. It is a pointless journey.
They'll never reach the top.

The doe stops midstride, midlife;
legs freeze-framed in circular stance
before time's on-going moment.

The ravens bark at the buzzard and shoo him away.
He deigns. Doesn't rush.
If I must, I will go – he seems to say,
but languidly, and in my own time.

The sky is cloud clear.
A perfect pitch of blue.
The silt settled in the storm-stirred stream.

Someone has poured petrol over the gorse.
In the March sun's sear
it is lit all over, goes up like hot fat,
a torch of tiny flames.

Red Brick Farm

The field is furrowed,
orderly manicured like Zen gravel.
No rain. And the swathed soil
has set to a cookie crust.

The red brick farm sits centrally,
a hub for the field's wheel
the noosing river, a May moon
pale and undistinguished,

behind, a long treeless ridge,
but for two battalions of squared-off fir,
ducking a steel girder of cloud.
The sun strikes and charges,

but the well grouped firs are firm.
They keep secrets and a night's dark
within their great thick coats.
They have long hidden pockets.

The river Wye out-pours;
far back on Plynlimon mountain a water jug has toppled:
here, nearing the end of their descent,
the waters stretch and glide.

The fidgeting trout leap acrobatically.
Under an alder on fist-sized stones
a heron holds the hour.
His dagger stabs the water with just one cut.

The Move

My mother moved for the first time in twenty-three years;
said goodbye in the last locking of her cottage door
to their unshared retirement dreams.
A door Dad built from scratch, its wire pulley bell,
the planting of their silver-wedding-birch trees.
The ashes of her man sprinkled like fine fertiliser
near the fox's crossing, at the foot of the red oak
with its man-sized leather-gloved leaves.

I noticed, too, looking from the back bedroom window
of her new build home, that the jackdaws
were moving far faster than intended:
left the branch, and were cast up, unannounced,
by a hightailing estuary wind; fast-forwarded beyond themselves
with a sea-bore surge, a sudden thrust and push.

Profusion

Pushed or pulled the growth of your life?
The grass gives way to weeds.
The dandelions like a massed tribe
came, camped and now have gone.
The clover cross-stitches, multiplies its lattice,
raises up putty-white pompoms,
something for the bees. The spider starts to spin,
into summer's depths a thickening, a deepening.
The earth's riches, its priceless hoards
unstoppable, inexhaustible. The brambles bend.
The lupins and foxgloves go up like skyscrapers.
And everything in your life is unstoppable too.
This force fuses you. Makes some days difficult.
So much of it. You don't know what to do.

Midsummer

The year gets over its bump start.
Now scuttles along. Traffic trains and trams.
Outdoor concerts come then go.
The trees hulk; grow more lubberly
and more muscular; more certain of themselves,
sculpted and weighted as bronze casts.

Midsummer surprises. Days fuse nights,
unsheathed in an openness, an un-sheeted-ness,
earth with its wide-eyed lightness,
its stratospheric unroofed-ness.
                              Dusk dissolves;
peach then pinks; low lilac blurs to violet,
night barely covers. A thin shawl is all.

From Gaol Ferry Bridge above the trees,
as you weave your way back from the gig,
a solitary star stalls you; sparks the dark,
as though some stranger is drawing hard;
but that's no star, that flickering fag,
strobing, night-cuffed, is red planet Mars.

Glass

My father fist-hearted,
blunted, crushed, gave no ground.
Stuck like that granite boulder
we stumbled upon in Pembrokeshire
adrift in a cliff-top field.
A beached stone
that hadn't budged
for five million years.
Looking on, I finally grasped
the weight we'd been under,
the obstruction.
Others, you see,
walkers, the farmer, the sallying sheep
had steered a small, scarred path around it.
He took his heaviness
to the intensive care bed;
lay cold and motionless
after the operation had gone badly,
ventilated, transfused then later dead.
Yes, we wept.
I think now, if we can't change
we can't live, if our stones won't crack,
we'll never reveal the mineral elegance
of our best most colourful parts:
cavities of surprising crystal,
the lights of our rare coloured glass.

Repose

I am as patient as the bees in my garden.
I have cut the stamp-sized lawn with a strimmer.
I have raked the damp clots into heaps
like swept shorn hair in a barbers;
I have bagged it in ASDA carriers to dispose of later.
Shoved it in like a devalued currency.
I have started to pull at the weeds, celandine,
a bright blanket of yellow flowers
and uncovered what I planted last year: ferns
under the elder, lupines and a single foxglove
urgently replicating. I go to my garden
as to the Delphic Oracle; one way to know myself.
I step back, sit silent in my rickety chair.
The ants have opened their motorway along the red bricked stair.

Brunel's Bridge at Dusk

The wood's colours drain
as though someone has pulled
an earth-sized plug

or flicked a key on Photoshop;
clambering cliff-edged greens
now a drear upholstered brown.

The lights of cars roll over Brunel's bridge
like marbles, bright one-way eyes;
swimming body-less in the dusk.

In the river at the bottom of the gorge,
lost on the cars and their passengers,
a wood-shaved spring moon bathes,

a thumb-width wider than the one in the sky,
like an old ferryman leaning on his paddle –
slowly crossing to the other side.

The Other Room

A couple of better nights in the spare room,
the office, my son's room when he stays,
snug on the flotsam futon bed
tucked to the sill of the door-sized window,
the sky now towering above his dad's head
like a steeple, and me, as a boy again,
lost in the liquorice dark's close comfort,
the locked stopped hours of the clock,
the weightless, graphite bright night,
and my parents, and my sister, and the dogs
in the hall and the tarry day is done, and me,
radiantly awake, frocked in my dark night imagination,
sleepless as an owl, watching out, wide-eyed,
flying hedgerows, and the fields' grey ghosts outside.

Bike

I sold the sleek black bike
you said I should buy;
my special treat,
in the shop on my own I couldn't fulfil.
It took your love,
your woman's will
to tutor me in the art of self-giving
and not to fear the things that feed.
Self-denial father's handed down creed.
Cycling was the emblem of our in-love fun.
We headed out evenings after work,
met near the deer park,
rode out that summer to an unending, un-setting sun.
What now our love is done?

The Gate

The moon leans into the courtyard
like a farmer looking over a gate.
One last cloud hovers, a thin chicken
wishbone in the dusk sky.

In the amethyst dark the courtyard
shadows drain; slaking off the wall
of the sand-brick house,
slipping over the shale to climb
the barn's hidden wall.

The umbrella holly tree is canonised.
The white cast-iron gate
sheens a rare underwater coral,
it has never looked so brilliant, nor so central.
Something in the moon surprises,

the way it is there, uninvited,
the way it holds what it sees
and draws it skyward
like the twine of a bow
flexing the night that little bit closer.

The yard is not just the yard,
the sand-brick house not quite now a home,
the waiting gate no longer a passing place
but the entrance offered to an august world.

August

The weather is unseasonably cold,
the flat's floorboards cold. In the garden
the courgette flowers but fails to fruit.
The tomatoes hang green and heavy,
like water bombs. Everywhere the boughs bend,
the elder with its black-beaded bunches,
its little popping mice eyes.
The crooked old pear across the road
is having a stellar season, lit up
like a winter tree with row upon row
of olive-green light bulbs. No one comes
or the boughs are too high. In disgust
it is chucking them on the road.

Silent Windows

Back home from Crete to rain, the easyJet airbus
taxiing on the runway then the telltale flick
of pearls on the small oval windows.
Clouds smothering the land's ballooned greens
like an insulating jacket on a boiler.

Back to the flat, a poor light-leaked interior,
and the shut-in-ness of it, after two weeks out in sun,
the living room's sienna shadows,
the curled up leaves of houseplants, the unread paper,
where the world's news froze.

Back to the stasis of skies we've outgrown,
inky inching clouds, bilged with cargo,
tanked up, threatening, the wettest June on record.
Daily, the bruise is bled,
the land, that old musty prayer book it splatters on.

Back to knowing heaven's haul is incessant,
that time lumbers like a listless cloud,
mordant heavy, something for the scales,
something solid we weigh,
afternoon hours through silent windows.

Gran

After Grandpa died she sold the mock-Tudor house,
with the wide lawn and shade-giving cedar,
that backed on to the park, where her two girls
first rode a horse. In one retreating act
sealed off her lost love from the rest of her life.
She took to indoors, bought a seventh-floor flat
on the outskirts of town, watched Wimbledon
for forty more years on a walnut cabinet TV,
painted small, delicate wildflowers mid-afternoon,
on long, sleepless nights read biographies,
cooked reheated meals on her Belling hob,
the kitchen no bigger than her old larder.
And if she went out, she was a little winged bird,
she'd scurry off, all elbows, to do battle with the herd.

Glare

You pull the car over
in a confused funk
not knowing if you wish to vanish
aimlessly up the Welsh coast road,
or, if, in fact, you've got to the nowhere
your city-sapped mind
needed for a few days to find.

You pull the car over
because out of the clenched heart,
a phrase jumps clear, like a badger bolting
from a hedgerow; some seizure that names
in tide-turning fashion your fate.
All problems are problems of love
and love it's not possible to get above.

Voices

And we forget the dead once had voices,
and are not now living lives, but lie
under thickset slabs where the squirrels
scurry and forage in the urgent energies of autumn,
spinning acorns between fleet hands,
and the Rosebay willowherb, sunned-out,
casts its trains of silk-soft seeds
from fishing rod stems, bent bowing
to the stones of the sun-dappled wall.

And once they sounded as we do now
with heart and head and chord and lung,
the many millions may be gone from this earth
our hearing knows and summer's familiar tones.
Easy to forget then, in the Victorian grand tombs
of the cemetery garden and the fields and woods,
where we now run, with cackling magpie and crow,
under the charging same sun, which rounds
on our time too, that the dead once had voices.

Loch Broom

The low slung arms of land across the loch
are losing their shawls, fog slipping off the shoulders
slowly, like someone falling asleep.

Unblemished, Loch Broom is perfecting its morning mirror.
Cotton clouds dangle on threads
and the air patiently waits, set like gelatine.

The early hour will not hurriedly move –
this day, of all in the year, was a particularly easy birth.
Slipped out, like the ferry that leaves the harbour.

There is a sense in the slowness that not one tree
didn't sleep well. That even the land hit
the button of deep sleep, and wiped the past clean.

Cockermouth in October

Storms come in for several days at a time.
The weather is one large mopping,
the clouds slop on the landscape
and then from an invisible bucket refill
to the limit, this October the time
for a multiple wash, double spin
an earth rotational pay-load.

We hunker down, as with the town
our dimensions of space flat-ironed,
a bivariate horizon, green to overhang
grey, clouds as low as valley-skinning
fighter jets, risk-inclined. Yet the streets
have all the room they need to come clean.

The leaves are beyond use,
horsewhipped, sent harshly to town
and to town flayed castle walls,
turning in alleyway detention corners;
edging up to dustbins, mounting people's
front doors like shut-out cats.

The rest decant where they can, kerb rivulets,
drain gutters, boating in puddles,
black-hole pools, others I saw exodus
more quickly; sticker-stuck to the Cocker,
glissading at Main Street bridge
down the thick honey stream.

October

a new quarantine,
days that hold before the clocks change,
the summer air chills to a setting coolness
like a dish removed from the oven.

The earth is preparing
to become its own walk-in larder,
the heat of life turned down daily
by half degrees.

Some burly blacksmith
has quenched the sun
in the cold sea of the sky,
the cherry flames, distant, intensify.

Is that the sun setting
beyond the hill, or a fire
flaring the crooks
of the black ash trees?

Late Hour

We have found a new routine;
slightly earlier to bed, slightly less late talking
as we sink in this low-lying futon to dream.

The day slips off as easily as our clothes;
the heating makes a dull milk shed moan
and something outside our hilltop flat grows and grows.

Is it night? A star's tincture? The sense
of what we will not know? Our world
shrinks to the white width of the bedroom's lens.

Night thickens and the wall
listens. A desert sphinx, a blank Buddha,
it says nothing, a nothing, that is all.

Departure from Arnisdale

Not wanting to close the door
he left everything behind, cups,
papers, broken back chair
as it was, his living realm

and summered days but open to the wind.
He had always wanted this –
a world one day to leave behind
and to do it in such a way as to have

one known guest arrive; poured in sky
through an open doorway. I saw him
on his porch, head high to the low
door beam, poised, watching out

for the weather across the loch to clear
and seeing, I'm sure, the first wild salmon
return. The following day he left,
not wanting to close the door.

Acknowledgements

I'd like to thank the editors of the following publications for first giving these poems a home. *PN Review* ('October', 'Owl', 'Late Hour'); *The London Magazine* ('Home'); *The Spectator* ('Sea Bream Dinner', 'Loch Broom', 'Bike', 'Spring', 'August', 'Words', 'Black Knight', 'Starlings', 'Stalker'); 'Raceme' (Departure from Arnisdale – shortlisted for the Bridport Prize 2008, Gran); 'Ice Anthology', Pighog Press 2012, (December); 'The Echoing Gallery' anthology, Redcliffe Press, 2013 (Brunel's Bridge at Dusk); 'The Cockermouth Poets' Anthology 2012 (Cockermouth in October).

'Sea Bream Dinner' was runner-up in the Arvon International Poetry Competition 2010 and published in the competition anthology 2010 and re-published in *York Notes for GCSE: Unseen Poetry Study Guide*, York Notes/York Press. 'Raskolnikov' won the SaveAs Writers' International Poetry Competition 2016.

'Inselberg Father,' *From Glasgow to Saturn*, Glasgow University e-zine.

'Llandduesant,' was published online at New Boots and Pantisocracies: WN Herbert/Andy Jackson and then in the anthology of the same name published by Smokestack Books 2016.

Thanks to Eyewear Publishing for the pamphlet *Black Knight*, March 2016.

Thanks to Amy Wack and the Seren team for their passion and commitment; my Bristol poetry group The Spoke: Elizabeth Parker, Bob Walton and Claire Williamson; Rhian Edwards, Claire Williamson, Liz Lefroy for manuscript advice; Gwyneth Lewis; Rachael Boast; Julie-ann Rowell for her critical eye, steadfast encouragement in the early days and on-going belief, Jon Sen for housing me in a dark time, Joe, Maisie and Fiona and to my supportive mates especially those at Southville Running Club – may the miles keep coming.